DON'T EAT THE FROG

HELPFUL ADVICE FOR
WRITERS WITH ADHD &
OTHER BRAIN BEES

VICKY QUINN FRASER

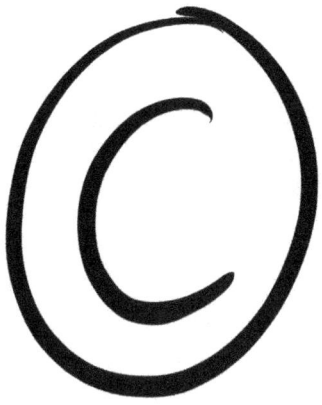

First published September 2023 by Moxie Books.

Copyright © 2023 by Vicky Quinn Fraser

Illustrations also copyright © 2023 by Vicky Quinn Fraser, although why you'd want to nick doodles of questionable quality, I've no idea.

All rights reserved. Some wrongs reserved, too.

You can't reprint or reproduce this book without written permission from me, on actual paper (or possibly a postcard). If you ask nicely, I might say yes.

Oh, and you can quote bits from it. Definitely. Especially if you're going to share them all over the internet and tag me.

ISBN:

Print: 978-1-8382513-4-5

Ebook: 978-1-8382513-5-2

Dear Reader

I'm a writer with ADHD[1] and for the longest time I thought I was a trash-panda because the usual writing and productivity advice doesn't work for me.

I don't want to eat the frog.

For a start, I'm vegetarian; plus I'm pretty sure I wouldn't like the texture.

Have you heard the productivity advice "eat the frog first"? I'd be surprised if you haven't. It's yelled at us from all corners of the internet and bookshops and online guru courses as the thing we absolutely must do if we want to succeed.

Want to maximise your productivity? Write all the books?

EAT THAT FROG.

---

1 I don't really like the term ADHD. It has the words "deficit" and "disorder" in it, and they're not fun labels to have. But I get why we use it. However, I describe myself thusly: I have bees in my brain. Like a big buzzy hive of chaos in there, it is. Also see: TV static.

It's all Mark Twain's fault. Kind of.

Back in the mists of time he apparently said, "Eat a live frog first thing in the morning and nothing worse will happen to you the rest of the day."

I mean, for most of us, he's probably not wrong—but this was in the days before rail replacement bus services so…

Then business gurus oozed their way into the world and co-opted Mark Twain's nifty little phrase, twisting it into productivity doctrine.

The frog became a metaphor for the most difficult or thorny or unpleasant, or even enjoyable!—but necessary—task on your to do list. And so the idea is that you do that first and the rest of the day will be easier.

At first glance, and for many people, that makes perfect sense.

As I'm sitting here typing, I'm nodding along even now and thinking, "Yes, yes. Do the hard thing first. That makes sense."

And yet…

And yet.

What actually happened when I tried to "eat the frog" was a whole lot of nothing followed by crippling shame.

And that wasn't all.

Nobody wants to do their taxes (except for weirdo accountant types), so procrastinating that task is understandable. But what about the things I WANTED to do?

The books I wanted to write?

The trapeze routines I wanted to create?

The house renovations I wanted to do?

The things I know—1,000% KNOW—I will delight in if I can only get started?

Yeah. It was a problem.

When faced with a hard thing I didn't want to do, or a hard thing I desperately wanted to do, the same result occurred: I would either stare at a wall getting more and more agitated, play a game on my phone getting more and more agitated, or impulsively learn how to play the ukulele while—you guessed it—getting more and more agitated.

So what was going on? Why couldn't I eat the frog like all the successful people? And why couldn't I do the things I knew would bring me joy?

Was I broken? Defective? Lazy? Useless? All of the above?

Took me decades to discover three things:

1. When most people say they're lazy, they mean they could do the thing if they wanted to, but they're choosing not to. I've spent my whole life saying I'm lazy when I've been trying desperately to do the thing but it's like a giant yeti is sitting on top of me,

preventing me from doing it. Or even moving.

2. I have ADHD,[1] which means I struggle to do even things I want to do, let alone boring stuff I don't want to do. Executive dysfunction is a bitch.

3. Most of the writing advice out there is written by neurotypical people for neurotypical people, without an ounce of empathy or consideration for those whose brains work differently. It's simply presented as truth by people (read rich white dudes) who are so used to having their opinions accepted as fact, it doesn't occur to them that they might be wrong, or that there might be another way of being in the world.

What's more, a lot of this advice isn't even great for people who AREN'T neurodivergent. It's just the way it's always been done.

Look at our sit-down-quietly-in-one-place-for-literally-hours-and-kill-off-the-hands-on-classes education system for a great example of things that don't work well for most humans, and yet we continue to do it anyway.

Trying to cram ourselves into boxes that aren't made for us is a fast-track to shame and burnout.

I've been a writer, one way or another, since I was around four years old and yet I've never felt like a writer. I felt like an outsider; a mess. As an adult, for the longest time, I felt like I was trying on someone else's clothes, and they were two sizes too small for me.

---

[1] And probably autism, too.

I had all these ideas; why couldn't I write? I have hundreds of abandoned writing projects languishing on my hard drive. I'd write fitfully, occasionally creating something I was proud of, but mostly buzzing through my days feeling like something crucial was missing.

I wanted to find that flow state successful writers talk about so often, but it eluded me. I seemed to lack the discipline to shepherd my ideas onto paper and see them through. I felt like a lazy, useless, fake failure.

When I got my ADHD diagnosis, things started to change. I began to see that maybe the world wasn't designed for people like me. And that by trying to squash myself into a neat little grey box when I'm shaped like a giant multicoloured ink splat, I was suffocating.

I began, slowly, to realise there are different ways of writing. Of not just struggling through the world, but soaring through it.

I began to find the joy.

That's where this MicroBook started: I began to find ways to do the things I want to do without burnout, shame, and a simmering sense of rage and loss.

I offer it up to you, dear reader, as a collection of suggestions, observations, and paths to joy if you feel you need a little help to write more freely and joyfully.

Or to create anything more freely and joyfully, really.

This book is aimed at writers, but it's not only for writers. It's for you, if you create things.

None of what follows is an instruction.

None of it is "the one true way to success".

It's simply what has helped me and my clients to create the things they want to create, and let go of some of the shame and frustration we've gathered along the way.

Let's find the joy!

TTFN,

Vicky Quinn Fraser

August 2023

The Dopamine Sandwich

Speaking of joy, have you tried a Dopamine Sandwich? It's where we sandwich the task we're avoiding between two slices of dopamine.

I'm no neuroscientist (obviously) but here's what I've figured out about my brain, and my theory as to why the Dopamine Sandwich works.

If someone (mostly me—I'm someone) tells me I must do the most difficult, misery-inducing task first, before anything else, and only then can I have a reward, I will almost certainly do nothing at all.

For hours.

And feel terrible about it.

Who wants to start their day like that? NOT ME.

I tried for years to work like this and felt like a horrible failure, trapped in a shame cycle that meant the more I tried to make myself eat the frog, the less able I was to do anything at all.

Until I realised it wasn't a rule.[1] Nobody will put me in prison if I choose to not eat the frog.

Instead, I discovered it was possible to trick myself into doing the thing I was avoiding by doing something that brought me pleasure first.

I could eat dessert before eating my vegetables—then get another helping of pudding afterwards. Yay!

For example: maybe I play Lemmings on my phone for 10 minutes. Or read a passage of a book I love. Or put on a tune and dance like a loon.

Then, when the dopamine is good and shiny, and I have a smile on my face, and I feel like I could do anything — I ride that wave right into my frog.

When I'm on that little high, full of energy and enthusiasm, I can point my bees in the direction I actually want to go in—and we're off!

Then, more often than not, I remember how much I enjoy doing the thing I was avoiding, and how much easier it is to do it than not do it.

(Unless it's taxes. Nobody enjoys taxes.)

Then I reward myself again with a little treat.

Dopamine. Frog. Dopamine.

---

1 The power of people with a big platform presenting their opinions as facts is HUGE. Because almost everything out there about productivity, business, art—it's opinion, or it's true only for a certain type of person, some of the time. But when it's presented with that level of confidence, we're all primed to believe it. It's dangerous.

The Dopamine Sandwich.[1]

Next time you're struggling to start a Hard Thing, make yourself a dopamine sandwich.

See if it works for you too.

---

[1] I have a theory that bread is made out of pure dopamine. I don't understand people who choose not to eat bread—allergies and illnesses aside. Why would you deny yourself such wondrous delights?

So small you can't fail

You cannot climb a mountain in a single leap, grasshopper.

You cannot write a book in a single sitting.

Do not set out to climb the mountain; start by putting on some pants.

Do not set out to write your book; start doodling with your idea.

Make your next step so small you cannot fail.

Sort your space out

I have many infuriating habits but I think the one that drives Joe[1] most up the wall is my penchant for using every available horizontal surface as a filing cabinet.[2]

I don't mean to do it; it just happens.

Because my brain knows that if something is put away tidily, I will forget it exists; the horizontal filing is like my working memory. It's a thing I'm constantly working on, and when we have a house that is not a building site, I'll devise a system where I can label everything so I know where it is.

The super-frustrating thing is: I hate mess. HATE IT. I find it supremely stressful.

So you can imagine how upsetting it is to be both the cause of the mess and the victim of it.

---

1 Joe is the world's best husband: fact.
2 When I moved out of my parents' home, they used to joke that the thing they missed most about my presence was the pint glasses half-filled with water I'd scatter around the house.

Except in my office.

That drives Joe round the bend too: he comes into my office and sees it pristine: tidy bookcases, neat piles of books I'm actually using, and only useful things I need on my desk.

Why can't I be like this in the rest of the house?

That's a good question, and I'll ponder it at length, sometime.

But for now, here's why my office is super tidy: because if it's not, I cannot get anything done for two reasons:

1. The aforementioned supreme stress of being in a messy environment.
2. The distraction. I will definitely avoid doing the hard thing I want to do if there's a thousand things that catch my eye that might entertain me briefly.

So, my writing space is tidy.

If you struggle to get started or stay focused, look at your environment: is it conducive to calm, to focus, to getting shit done? If not, what can you do to make it so?[1]

---

[1] My friend Hannah de Keijzer has a brilliant service called Feel Good Where You Write, and she'll help you sort your space out and make it writer-brain-friendly.

Working memory

How many tabs are open on your internet browser right now? There are 27 open on mine right now, and that's not that many for me.

I figured out this is because it's where I store my working memory. I have an idea or a thought or a question, so I type it into a search engine, open a new tab, and leave it there so I can come back to it later.

This stresses Joe out too, he says I'm a messy browser, but that's okay because he can mind his business on his tidy laptop and I'll mind mine.

I do have a little hack though: I use OneTab and Toby and that helps me keep my tabs under control.

At the end of each day, I click my little OneTab icon and it sucks all the open tabs into a list and stores them by day—so I can just scroll through for that thing I know I found a couple of weeks ago, but then didn't do anything with.

And Toby is like an organiser for all the websites I use most often—but also for interesting things I find. I can categorise them and save them and come back to them. List websites are great here because I often want interesting stories and facts and snippets, so I have a bunch of sources for that kind of thing.

A tidy browser is an empty mind, I say—so let your browsing go wild, find your inspiration—but make sure you don't stress about losing ideas. Find a way to keep the tabs under, well, tabs.

Wormholes

I'll just check this George Orwell quote and find out how he used to publish his essay pamphlets.

Three hours later: I am now something of a minor expert on whirlpools.[1]

Research can be an infuriating process for me because I will go off on a dozen side-quests while trying to find what I need. In this, the internet has not been my friend. But I also don't want to lose those side-quests completely because a lot of my ideas come from my distractibility.

So here's what I do:

I write down exactly what I need to know in bullet points—the gaps in my knowledge that are preventing me from making progress on my book or article or whatever.

I set a time limit, say 30 minutes, to find the info I need.

---

[1] The biggest and most spectacular are the Corryvreckan in the western isles of Scotland, the Naruto Strait in Japan, the Old Sow and Skookumchuck Narrows in Canada, and Moskstraumen and Saltstraumen in Norway. You're welcome.

Every time I see something interesting but irrelevant, I open a tab and save it in OneTab or Toby[1]—I don't have to follow that thread now, I can save it for later.

Timer goes off, I have a little dance break, then I turn off the internet, take my research, and do my writing.

If I find I need to do more research, I'll make a note of it and come back to it later, in another research session.

It's not foolproof, but it does significantly cut down on my absolute nonsense and it allows me to indulge my fascination for everything that comes my way. Win win!

---

1 Browser tidies that I use to keep my working memory intact, so in three months I will know exactly where to find that page on emu eggs I stumbled across while researching how to use syllepsis.

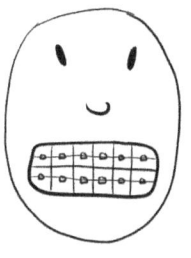

"You can't write & never will"

I run an enchanting little course called MicroBook Magic, in which people with short little attention spans and a tendency to flightiness—or people who for whatever reason believe that writing A Big Book is beyond them—write a book.

A MicroBook.

More on this later, because for right now I just want to say: sometimes adults bloody SUCK. One of my clients wrote me a beautiful testimonial after writing her MicroBook with me, but in it, she said this:

"I double majored in college—English & Psych, but had a writing professor who said I 'couldn't write & never would'. So I just assumed it was a talent I didn't have."

If anyone has ever told you something like that—about writing or anything else—try to remember this: it's their opinion. And a shitty opinion at that. Anybody can become good at writing; some can become great: it takes practice. But who the hell is going to practice if someone has told them they can't write and never will?

Well, my amazing client, for one.

If I'd been told that as a child or a young adult, I don't know if I'd be doing what I do now because that kind of rejection hurts.

Rejection sensitivity dysphoria (RSD) is a real thing. I suffer terribly from it. If you have ADHD, chances are you have it too. We put far too much store on what other people say and think of us. The things people say—and the cringey[1] things we do—stick with us vividly.

As soon as I could afford it, I spent thousands rearranging my teeth because of something a grown man said to me when I was a teenager. I wouldn't smile in photos for years. I hate photos of myself. And the stupid thing? That man was WRONG.

Just like my client's professor was wrong.

Be careful who you listen to and what you take on board. Treat what you hear as a single data point. Keep a folder of praise and lovely things people have said and read it often, because despite what gurus online might say about external validation, most of us need some of it, because we live in the world with other people and we are more-or-less human.

---

1 They feel cringey to us—even if nobody else notices. I will wake up at 3am worrying about something "stupid" I did five years ago. Fun times!

A MicroBook?

What's a MicroBook, you're probably not asking? It came from a conversation with my friend Misty. I'm pretty sure we share a brain. She's definitely my sister from another mister.

I was wailing about how I was struggling to find people who wanted to join my Weird + Wonderful Book Society 3-month book writing programme, which went brilliantly the first couple of times I ran it during the Covid lockdowns, then fizzled out.

What was going on?

I don't know, but Misty suggested I take my own advice and make it so small I couldn't possibly fail. Not a normal-sized book, but a really small one.

"A MicroBook?" I suggested.

"Exactly that!" she agreed.

Ten minutes later, I outlined what it'd be and what I'd offer.

Two days later, MicroBook Magic was born.

One week later, I had 10 people ready to write a MicroBook with me. None of them really knew what a MicroBook was. Nor did I, quite, yet. But I knew it'd be brilliant.

I define a MicroBook as fewer than 100 pages, and probably fewer than 80. Somewhere between 10 and 25,000 words, but maybe less if you're adding illustrations or it's a graphic book or a poetry compendium. And possibly physically small, too.

Because who says a "proper book" has to be 300 pages and 60,000 words?

The traditional publishing industry, that's who. It's a convention they have because it's a convention. They do it that way because that's the way it's always been done.

But why?

No idea.[1] But I know what it leads to: bloated, fluff-filled books that could have been half the size, or a third of the size, or even just the first couple of chapters. Books padded out to meet the arbitrary requirements of an old-fashioned industry that insists on locking authors into contracts that might not suit them.[2]

Screw that.

---

[1] Okay part of the reason is if a book is under 100 pages it can be difficult to put words on the spine. But that's not always a consideration.

[2] Hashtag not all big books, obvs. There are loads of brilliant 300-page books out there. I'm talking about the ones that are 80% fluff, and there are a LOT of them too.

Write the book that makes sense for you, and if that's 10 pages long—well, you're in good company. George Orwell wrote some cracking MicroBooks—called pamphlets back then—that changed the world in tiny ways.

Just read his *Politics & the English Language* and you'll see what I mean—his MicroBook drew attention to the way politicians use language to obfuscate and mislead. As relevant today as it was back then, yes?

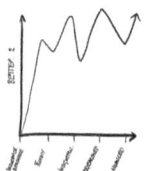

What does "better" mean?

People often tell me they want to become a better writer.[1] I see courses and teachers out there that promise to make us better writers. And the question I always ask is:

Better *how*?

In what way?

Compared to what?

"Better" doesn't mean anything, on its own, so let's define it clearly so we know what we want to get better *at*. Because if we don't, we'll spiral into vague wormholes in which we try to hit a fuzzy target that keeps moving. Not good for people who already struggle to stay on track.

Like, do you want to be funnier? More poignant? Less waffley? More insightful? Less self-centred?

Do you want to write vividly visual scenes, or sensory

---

[1] If you're a singer, artist, musician, engineer, inventor, dancer, coder, creator of any kind, I hope this will help you, too.

delights? Do you want to learn how to use metaphor and simile effectively?

Do you want to write impactful beginnings and memorable endings?

Do you want to write wonderful observational essays, à la David Sedaris? (Me too, friend, me too.)

There are so many ways we can become better but none of them will happen unless we know what we mean by "better." So start there.

Why do you write?

That's a good question to ask yourself, from time to time. The answer will almost certainly change; it does for me.

I write because I can't not write. I write because it helps me to think. I write because it's fun, and challenging, to see what I can do if I put this word here, and this one just over here, leaning against the bookcase, and that one

    THERE

                    right in the middle of the floor.

What does it create?

Anyway—back to you.

Why do you write?

Is it something you feel you have to do, to earn a crust? Or is it something you want to do, long to do, yearn to do? Or a bit of both?

There's no wrong or right answer, just the truths. More than one of them, depending on the day, and season, and mood.

And now another question…

How do you feel when you write?

This, too, will depend on what you're doing, why, when, where, and how. That's a lot of Ws all in a row, but they're useful Ws that can help us figure out what's going on in our pages and in our heads.

How do you feel when you write? When you create?

Try to create a habit of scribbling your mood in your margin when you write something (digitally or analoguely[1]) and then look back at it from time to time. What were you feeling when you wrote this? Or that? How do those pieces differ? How does your mood influence your writing?

When I am angry, I find that my ideas are interesting, spiky, if incoherent. They make a good base to come back to when I have calmed down, which is usually by the time I've finished writing out my rage.

---

[1] Is analoguely a word? No matter, it is now. Make up words if you like.

When I'm hungry, I can't. I panic, get overwhelmed, and nothing makes much sense.

When I'm tired, obscure images and memories float up from just beneath the surface, and when I find them later, I usually have something to play with.

When I'm happy, I use a lot of exclamation marks, and I LIKE THEM!!!

When I'm overwhelmed or afraid, writing calms me, because nothing is ever as bad as it feels when you have it imprisoned inside your skull.

When I'm sad, I revert to my teenage emo self and I usually can't bear to look at what I've written. But sometimes I find the germ of an idea in there, and I water it, and see what happens.

Can you spot any patterns? Do you struggle to write when you're hungry? Tired? Angry? Sad? Happy? Overwhelmed? Excited?

Make up words

Marvapotamus is one of my favourite words. I wish I could say I made it up, but I didn't. An old friend did. Now it's mine, because I use it all the time.

Here's one of mine: *snoozle*. This is what my cat, Noodle, does when he's on my knee. It's more than a snooze but less than a full-on sleep and it's very specific to him, because he covers his nose with his paw.

A bit later in this book you'll find another word I made up, which, if you have ADHD, will probably sound very perfect for you.

You're allowed to make up new words, you know. Anything you like. If there isn't a word for what you need, create a new one.

See if you can make "fetch" happen.[1]

---

[1] I asked Joe to read this first draft, and he added this note: "Fetch isn't going to happen, Gretchen." Are you a *Mean Girls* fan?

You don't want it badly enough

"If you haven't written a book yet, you just don't want it badly enough."

Ugh.

UGH, I say again, louder and more emphatically.

This is a trend that has spilled over from the wellness industry (which, ironically, is one of the most toxic cesspits around, together with the diet industry) and into the rest of the business world. This idea that we can "manifest" results out of our butts and that if something doesn't work for us, it's entirely our fault because we're broken or we don't want it enough.

Never mind that the programme or course was shitty or just not designed for certain brains to navigate. (I mean, that's fine, you can't design for everyone, just don't lie to us about it and say 'this'll work for everyone' when it clearly won't.)

Honestly, some people don't really want to write a book. Those people will probably never even think about writing a book; or if they do, it'll be fleeting and they'll forget about it and do something that matters more to them. But if you're here, reading this, and you desperately want to write a book but you just can't, then I promise you, it's not because you don't want it badly enough.

So, why haven't you written a book yet?

I don't know. But it would seem like a good idea to find out…

So... why haven't you written a book yet?

Have you asked yourself that question? I'm not being snarky; most people don't ask this question of themselves. Mostly, most of us will try to do something, fail, then just think, 'Oh well that's not a thing I can do, I guess.'

The whole of Western society and education (at least when I was at school) was set up to have us believe these things. That if we got the answer wrong, that was A Bad Thing, and if we get the answer right, then we're Good Children. Saying 'I don't know' was unthinkable because you'd get that look of disappointment or anger from the teacher or a parent. School wasn't about learning, it was about getting things right.

And there are now far too many adults running businesses or in positions of authority who loathe saying 'I don't know' so much they give (and sell) poor advice rather than admit they don't know something, and go and find out. Just look at our politicians.

The upshot of all this is that we try a thing, find we can't do it, decide we're not good at that thing, accept it at face value, and move on.

How about, instead, we get curious. Oh, I haven't written a book yet, but I really really want to. Why haven't I? Maybe grab a pen or your voice recorder app and mull it over.

If you're still stumped, try these questions on for size: do you have an idea you want to write about? Are you afraid your idea isn't good enough? Are you worried someone else has said it all already? Do you have literally no idea where to start? Or how to write a book at all? Are you worried you're not a good enough writer? Do you believe you don't have the time? Or energy? Or knowledge?

Have a think. See where you end up. Then, perhaps, you'll be ready to get going.

If not, read the next section.

Actually read the next bit anyway because I guarantee this is also getting in the way of you creating the things that are important to you.

You don't have to write to write

I have a friend and client—a genius brain coach[1]—who also has an interesting brain. She writes most of her work on her phone while walking around. Sitting at a desk doesn't work for her. She taps away in her Notes app or in Google Docs, then edits it all later.

I'd like to do this because I prefer stomping around while I think, too. But I find phones infuriating to write on.

Mostly because my autocorrect has decided I often use words like "OSS" and "ducking" and "and's". I mean, "and's"?[2] Wtf is that? I've never typed that in my life.

So I spend a lot of time swearing instead of writing, and that doesn't work for me.[3]

---

1 You should follow her on Instagram @jocelthem

2 Update: I'm now on the final edit and typesetting and my phone has decided to forget that "to" is a word and instead I mean "too". Or, inexplicably, "toooooooooooo".

3 Yes, I have tried resetting my dictionary and it won't reset. It just keeps all the bullshit it's decided I want to type.

But I do use my phone to write. I use the Voice Notes app allll the time, especially when I'm driving because I listen to a lot of podcasts and have ideas that I instantly forget if I don't write them down. It's easier now I have a smart watch because I can use that to record voice notes like I'm in Star Trek or some kind of spy, so I don't even have to faff with the phone.

Top tip: if you're recording ideas on Voice Notes, record a little context too. I can't tell you the number of ideas I listen back to and think, "I have no idea what I was on about here."

What other ways are there to write?

Scatter it to the winds

You don't have to have a dedicated Manuscript File to write a book.

There's a lot of advice out there about having a dedicated file for all your writing. Some people put it all in Word or a Google Doc. Others use software like Scrivener or Atticus or Ulysses or even Excel (I mean HOW).

My advice is always: use what you're comfortable with. And don't feel bad if it looks like an explosion in a confetti factory.

My books are often scattered everywhere: Scrivener, Notion, Google Keep, Voice Notes, my iPhone Notes App, paper notebooks, Post-It notes on a wall, my reMarkable, and 750Words.com. I know where most of it is. Every now and then I trawl through it and gather it together. And that's okay.

If I have to worry about finding the same document every time, I'll never write anything. And it'll get horribly confusing if it's one looooong doc. In the end, it all lands in Scrivener because I can put it all on virtual index cards and shift it around visually.

However you write, that's okay. Just write.

A WhatsApp poetry compendium

My friend Edd[1] moved to London and I miss him terribly. So every Friday (more or less—sometimes it's Saturday morning or even Sunday) we send each other a haiku.

Traditional Japanese poets would bristle at my description of what we write as "haiku" because strictly speaking, they're not. But they do follow the haiku technical form: 5-7-5.

Some of our haiku are genuinely beautiful.

Some of them are hilarious.

Some of them are gloriously terrible.

We were thinking we might publish them and illustrate them. Edd is a brilliant artist. I am an erratic artist. But we think it'll be fun, especially if he illustrates my haiku

---

1 You should definitely follow Edd on Instagram here: @eddstephen and marvel at his grace.

and I illustrate his.

The best thing about this whole thing is we're writing a little book of poetry by stealth. Via WhatsApp. So it doesn't feel like writing a book of poetry at all.

Ear-Cancelling Headphones

There's this episode of *Buffy the Vampire Slayer* in which Buffy accidentally acquires the ability to hear people's thoughts. It starts off as a quirky amusement; then all the people she loves start to avoid her, because who wants anyone to hear their innermost thoughts? And finally, she starts to lose her mind because she can't control it or shut it off. It's an endless cacophony in her head.

This is kind of how I feel when I'm in a noisy environment: battered from all sides by a physical torrent of noise I cannot shut off or filter out.

It's like TV static. Or a hive of bees in my head (hence why I call it bees in my brain).

I didn't realise other people could filter out background noise and focus on the thing they wanted to focus on until I was in my thirties. I thought I was just weak, short-tempered, anxious… a little pathetic. I had no idea I had auditory processing issues.

If I'm in my beautiful, calm office and the neighbours are blowing their fucking leaves around[1] or mowing their lawns or their dogs are barking, my stress levels rise and rise until I end up screaming or breaking something.

If I'm in a room with multiple conversations, I cannot follow any of them and have to leave before I scream.

And if I'm in a public place like an airport, it feels like torture. I feel like I am losing my mind.

Writing under these circumstances isn't just difficult for me; it's impossible. This kind of sensory overload is a large part of my inability to start or make progress on the things I want so badly to do, and I never realised it until a few years ago.

Then someone suggested buying some noise-cancelling headphones.[2] I'd been resisting for years because the good ones are very expensive and while I will happily splash money on some stuff, posh headphones weren't on my list.

More fool me because they're the best £279 I've spent in years. They have literally transformed my world from regularly unbearable to zen-like calm and a writing flow state I could only dream of before.

---

[1] If I were queen of the world, leaf blowers would be illegal, and their use result in being locked in a room full of fire ants and covered in jam. It's one of the "am I an arsehole" tests, like the trolley test: if you own and use a leaf blower I am very sorry to inform you that you fail the arsehole test.

[2] I keep accidentally calling them "ear-cancelling headphones" and I think I like that better

So if you struggle with auditory processing or distractions or sensitivity to sounds, my advice is: buy the absolute best noise-cancelling headphones you can afford.

The over-ear ones work best for me; the in-ear ones are all almost certainly designed for bigger male ears and are uncomfortable or painful, and they're just not as good.

Mine are Bose QuietComfort and they go everywhere with me. Give yourself the gift of silence if you're someone who cannot work with noise.

Then try out alpha wave music and rainstorms. Rainstorms are my preference, because they drown out whatever the noise-cancelling technology can't catch.

Fuck 5am

Around 2014, a couple of years into running my own business, I was still figuring out who I was and what I did and how I worked. I jumped on every piece of advice from people who looked shiny and successful, and tried it all.

I especially remember going through a phase of getting up at 5 am "to be more productive" and being thoroughly miserable because I am not a person who likes getting out of bed and frankly 5 am is night-time.

I did this for ages, shamed into it by "the 5 am club" whose message seemed to be that if one was truly serious about running a successful business and making one beeeeeeellion dollar, one had to get up at 5 am and cram raw kale into their faces. All that happened was I became a miserable person to be around and my eyes were carrying around the ugliest, biggest suitcases you've ever seen.

I crashed and burned, reader. I crashed and burned. And

I felt terrible about it because of course, if I couldn't get up at 5 am and do all the things, clearly I wasn't trying hard enough.

Well, that's bullshit.

If you love getting up at 5 am and that's when you do your best work—do that.

If you love getting up at midday and that's when you do your best work—do that.

Find your rhythm. Find your sweet spot. And do not let anyone else tell you that you "should" be doing it any other way. I tell ya, capitalism and puritanism has done a number on us: why do we have to be at our desks by 8am until 5pm, regardless of how much work we get done?

Pah. Find what works for you.

For me, right now, what works is getting out of bed between 6 and 6.15am, going for a 10-minute run before my body figures out what's going on, doing 10 minutes of yoga to stretch out, then having a shower and being at my desk with a mug of tea by 7am, at which point I write my morning pages on 750words.com.

These are my best days. Not necessarily my most *productive* days; but the days that I feel happiest and do the work I'm proudest of.

In a year, this routine will probably be different; I crave structure but I also get easily bored, so I change things up every now and then.

And that's okay too.

Write something shitty

Did you know that when an author publishes a book, it didn't always look like that?

Yes, but did you *really* know?

I have a theory, and it is this: we buy books from shops, and we read them, and we enjoy them or we do not. But we all accept that if this book has been published, it has met certain minimum standards. And so when we write a book we must meet them too.

And we must.

But not right away. Not on the first damn draft.

I think that somewhere in our subconscious minds we secretly believe that authors sit down and write a book all in one go and then they publish the book and then we read the book.

No.

That is not how this works.

All authors, everywhere, write books in stages and phases and the first draft is, at best, a mess; and at worst, it's a big pile of poo.

Remember that, and stop trying to write a perfect first draft because if you keep trying to write a perfect first draft, you'll never write *anything*.

Instead, try this little switcher:

Try to write something shitty. Make that your actual aim.

Go. Create shit.

Focus on direction, not destination

Speaking of goals… It's important to have them. We won't get anywhere if we don't know where we're going, as Yogi Berra said.[1]

But once I've set a goal, I take my eye off it, cos otherwise I'm aiming to write a great big fat finished book and that's just not gonna happen—keeping the focus on it can be very overwhelming for me.

So I keep my eyes on what I'm doing right now.

One word in front of another.

Every now and then I glance up and check I'm on track—or course correct if my ideas are changing—but I keep my eyes on what I'm writing.

Writing is an emergent property, and the destination changes as I create. I find where I'm going as I go along.

---

[1] Actually he said: "If you don't know where you're going, you might not get there" which always makes me snortle.

As E. L. Doctorow says, "Writing is like driving at night in the fog. You can only see as far as your headlights, but you can make the whole trip that way."

Chaos editing

They tell you: don't edit as you write. And, yes, that is good advice if you can manage it, but I often cannot manage it, because I write (and read) somewhat chaotically.

As I write, I also scan back up the page to what I've just slapped down. I'm mentally editing as I write, and if I see a typo up there, it pokes at me.

It can be supremely frustrating… and it can also be a fun way to get my ideas out. Because as I scan back up, it sparks new ideas I can splurge as I'm writing. It makes for a somewhat chaotic first draft, but by the time I've finished cutting and pasting and dragging stuff around, it's not in bad shape.

Sometimes I try to cover the screen and just write.

But often I simply cannot do that, so I embrace the chaos and see what falls out of my brain.

And, you know, writing without editing is just not how

a lot of writers write. For some of us, it goes something like this:

- Do almost anything except write for at least 30 minutes.
- Faff at the desk.
- Think. Doodle. Make notes.
- Write a handful of sentences.
- Get up and faff some more.
- Mess around with the sentences.
- Write a bunch more sentences, and mess with them too.
- Maybe find a flow state and hammer out an absolute river of drivel.
- Mess with it.
- Fin.

And that's fine. Your process will be different and that's fine too. You just need to find it.

And get words on paper, somehow, anyhow.

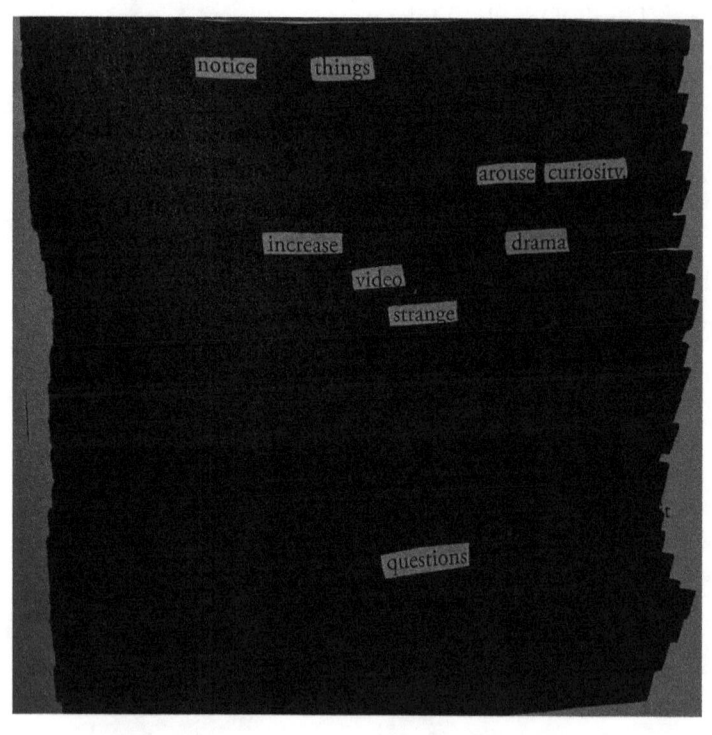

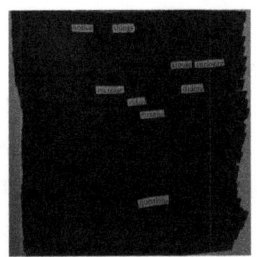

Newspaper blackout poetry

This isn't my idea—it's an old idea; 250 years old, I have recently learned. But I learned it from Austin Kleon, one of my favourite creativity peeps.

It's in his creativity journal, the *Steal Like an Artist Journal*. I open it randomly when I'm feeling uninspired, and one day out popped a couple of pages from *Moby Dick*, photocopied onto the page. The prompt was: black out one word at a time until you're left with a poem.

I didn't know where to start.

Then I realised it didn't matter, and started anyway.

It was lots of fun and I "wrote" a cute little poem, and it's now a thing I do regularly. I do it with books I don't like because I am a terrible, terrible person. I also do it with misery letters from misery institutions like banks, governments, and utilities providers. I like to turn bureaucratic woe into art.

This is all by way of saying, if you're stuck, try something else. If all the prompts and writing advice and productivity sausages aren't working for you right now, and your executive dysfunction is strong and your enthusiasm is low, take something that already exists and turn it into something else.

That way, you don't have to start from scratch. You don't have to start at all. Someone has already started for you.

In fact, start here. With this piece! I've included it twice, just in case you don't want to transform the only version of this little story into some blackout poetry.

Flip the page; start blacking out words; see what you're left with.

Then send me a picture.

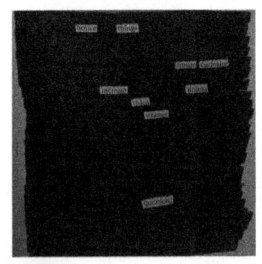

YOUR newspaper blackout poetry

This isn't my idea—it's an old idea; 250 years old, I have recently learned. But I learned it from Austin Kleon, one of my favourite creativity peeps.

It's in his creativity journal, the *Steal Like an Artist Journal*. I open it randomly when I'm feeling uninspired, and one day out popped a couple of pages from *Moby Dick*, photocopied onto the page. The prompt was: black out one word at a time until you're left with a poem.

I didn't know where to start.

Then I realised it didn't matter, and started anyway.

It was lots of fun and I "wrote" a cute little poem, and it's now a thing I do regularly. I do it with books I don't like because I am a terrible, terrible person. I also do it with misery letters from misery institutions like banks, governments, and utilities providers. I like to turn bureaucratic woe into art.

This is all by way of saying, if you're stuck, try something else. If all the prompts and writing advice and productivity sausages aren't working for you right now, and your executive dysfunction is strong and your enthusiasm is low, take something that already exists and turn it into something else.

That way, you don't have to start from scratch. You don't have to start at all. Someone has already started for you.

In fact, start here. With this piece! I've included it twice, just in case you don't want to transform the only version of this little story into some blackout poetry.

Flip the page; start blacking out words; see what you're left with.

Then send me a picture.

Fuck the grammar police

Did you know grammar changes? Words change, too. So next time somebody gleefully points out a grammar mistake, or tells you that your dialect is "incorrect", hand them a copy of the original *Beowulf* and ask them to read it out loud.

Because that was "correct" English once, too.

How about Chaucer? Or Shakespeare? Both "correct" English.

In fact, Shakespeare made up tons of stuff and our English now looks and sounds like this largely because of his inventiveness and disregard for "rules."

The Victorians made up our current grammar rules and we all know how much fun that load of misery-bears were.

Our language has changed, almost beyond recognition, and it will continue to do so. There are loads of things the kids say that I do not understand at all, like, "He ate it all up, zaddy. No crumbs." Um, wut?

The only languages that don't change are dead ones, like Latin and ancient Egyptian.[1]

Embrace your linguistic quirks and dialectical phrases; they're part of what make your writing uniquely you. Especially if you're from a marginalised group. Do not let anyone try to erase your identity.

And don't listen to the dusty old English teachers and crusty old dudes who tell you you're wrong. You're probably not. And even if you actually are and your sentence makes no sense, that's what editors are for.

---

1 I learned how to read and write hieroglyphs at uni. I've forgotten most of it now but I've still got my Egyptian grammar books. Might dig 'em out and write a book in ancient Egyptian...

Go for a wee!

Next time you feel like an absolute trash-panda for procrastinating on something you really want to do, remember this:

I regularly procrastinate going for a wee. That's how strong my procrastination game is.

Which means a panicky dash through my garden, skidding to a halt in the nick of time, almost crying with relief.

Why am I like this?

So go, write the thing you want to write, but make sure you don't need a wee. It's really difficult to concentrate.

A jar of lemon curd & a spoon

"Are you okay?" Joe asked. I was curled in a foetal position on my rug, shaking and crying. "What happened?"

"I don't feel very well," I whimpered. "I feel shaky and sick and like the world is going to end. Is the world going to end?"

"I don't think so," said he. "What have you eaten today?"

Aha. I have eaten a jar of lemon curd. Out of the jar, with a spoon. I basically ate a jar of sugar and went about my business.

This used to happen a lot, and in my defence it's because of three things:

1. Our kitchen is a vile hellscape that makes me feel like my skin is going to crawl off my body so I don't want

to be in there for more than 7 minutes at a time.[1]

2. I am very busy with lots of things to do, some of which are even useful things I want to do at the time, so I don't have time to make actual food.

3. I forget eating food is a thing.

Lemon curd is a terrible lunch for anybody but it's doubly terrible for ADHD brains because of complicated nutrition and brain chemistry reasons I won't attempt to tackle here. Suffice it to say, the jar of lemon curd was the nadir of an increasingly dire spiral of food choices I'd made recently, and Joe decided to step in.

(I should say here that Joe does all the cooking in our house because he is amazing and also because he doesn't get distracted and destroy all our pans.)

Mostly, now, Joe makes enough dinner the night before that there's a portion left for me, so all I have to do is throw it in the microwave at lunchtime and BANG: a healthy and delicious meal that takes me 3.5 minutes to make. Only half the maximum time I can spend in our hellscape kitchen at a pop.

Funnily enough, my work has become more interesting, less stressful, and more creative since I started eating properly. Wonder why…

---

[1] We're not disgusting humans I promise; we're in the middle of renovating our cottage and the kitchen will happen at some point. I hope.

Warning: This chapter contains nuts

So, after the leftovers... Nuts are my secret brain weapon.

I don't always eat lemon curd out of the jar. Sometimes, if there are biscuits around, I'll shovel them into my face frantically, which is a terrible plan because there's a big buzz and then a catastrophic crash.

Then, one day at my hairdresser's house, I got the shakes because I had forgotten to eat in the mad rush to get there on time. She presented me with a bag of nuts and said she always keeps them around the house for just this eventuality.

So now that's my strategy too. Every week when we do our meal planning and online food shop, we add a couple of bags of mixed fruit and nuts to the list, and they come to live in my office.

During an Introduction to Pottery day, I made a rustic bowl, which is the perfect size for said fruit and nuts. And so now I munch on those all day and there's much less whimpering.

Plus nuts are good brain food because they are protein-rich, and help to make neurotransmitters, and can also prevent surges in blood sugar which can lead to ridiculous internet impulse purchases.

Try keeping a stash of nuts in your writing area and dig into them often, so on those days when you forget that food is a thing, you won't disintegrate like a wet flannel.

(**Note:** do not do this if you're allergic to nuts. Tasty alternatives: roasted chickpeas, wasabi peas, pumpkin seeds, Bombay mix if you're feeling retro.)

Day Themes

Mondays are just for me. They're for me to write. I have no client calls, I do no client work, I make no exceptions because when I do make exceptions, everything is terrible.

Here's an example: a client couldn't make any of my usual call days or times, and because I am a chronic people pleaser, I made an exception and booked her in for a Monday afternoon, thinking it would be fine.

Narrator: it was not fine. In fact, the call didn't even happen.

Because my brain knows that Mondays are my days, and I do not do client calls, so even though it was in my electronic calendar, I failed to write it down on my paper to do list, and for whatever reason, my watch didn't buzz me just before the call.

So I just… didn't show up.

Then didn't even understand the message I got from the client asking where I was, because there was no possible way for me to have missed a meeting. She was very understanding, but I was mortified.

And this is why I theme my days, and have strict rules about what I will and won't do, and when.

It's not me being an inflexible sod; it's me protecting myself *and* my clients from my bees, which are continually doing their damnedest to derail me.

The passive-aggressive post-it note wall

Sometimes I can't write the things I want to write because there is too much life admin taking up space in my head. And seeing it all on my to-do list, day after day, still undone is depressing.

It's a reminder of how incapable of adulting I am sometimes.

So I took all the things off my to-do list and put them into the real world, on my Post-It Note wall.[1]

Things like: book car into garage before exhaust falls off. Rebook dentist appointment. Sort birthday cards and gifts for family + friends. Book car MOT.

They're all on colourful Post-It notes and they're all

---

[1] One of my clients, Kelly, said she had no space on her walls for post-it notes, so I suggested she make herself a passive-aggressive advent calendar. Pick a picture she liked, then cover it with post-it instructions. Every time she does a task she's been avoiding, she gets to uncover more of the picture, until eventually she can see the whole thing again. Hurrah!

things that will take less than 10 minutes (in theory). So if I find myself with a few minutes, I can choose one, and do it, and take the Post-It Note away.

BUT THAT'S NOT ALL.

On the back of each Post-It is a treat! For example, at the time of writing this, I'm trying to get my bees to book my car into the garage so the exhaust doesn't fall off and when I do it—I get to book myself a few days in Edinburgh, on my own, to focus on doing things I really want to do but am struggling to get to.[1]

Gameify your adulting.

Create more time for writing.

Winning!

---

[1] By the time I wrote this, I had abandoned that car, bought one with a solid exhaust, and gone to Santorini instead because it was cheaper for me to fly to Santorini than get a train to Edinburgh and if that's not fucked up I don't know what is.

Habit stacking

I always wanted to be a writer who got up early and wrote stuff, but instead I'd hit snooze 53 times then skid to my desk for my first call, hair on fire.

This made me sad and anxious, so something had to change.

I read *Atomic Habits* by James Clear (it's so good) and decided to try habit stacking.

I want to exercise first thing in the morning and I want to improve my flexibility, so here's my first habit stack:

1. Fall out of bed and straight into running clothes.

2. Brush teeth, stagger out of the door and run for 10 minutes.

3. Straight into office where my yoga mat is already laid out[1] for 10 minutes of yoga or 30 minutes of flexibility training, depending on the day.

---

[1] I design my environment, too. More on that shortly…

I stack those three things together so I don't have to think about them or argue with myself.

Next habit stack:

1. Shower.

2. Make tea.

3. Write 750 words while drinking tea.

4. Journal with coloured pens and fun.

These three things go together, too.

Putting out the laundry goes together with cleaning out the chickens' coop, so they both get done.

Running my Creative Playground sessions goes with working on my current book project.

Stack together the things you want to do, but struggle to do. And read *Atomic Habits*.

De-friction your life

I am very easily distracted by pretty much anything, so I have to design my life in such a way that there's very little friction.

I don't have to spend time choosing and finding running clothes in the morning, by which time I'll have talked myself out of it—they're already laid out waiting for me.

I don't have to clear space and drag my yoga mat out each morning—I do that the night before when I leave my office, so I have no excuse to not stretch.

I have my day planner ready and 750words.com opens up as soon as I open my browser, so I don't get distracted with other websites.

How can you reduce friction?

Just move your body

I got the best piece of advice about getting unstuck, from listening to a podcast.[1]

Britt Frank, who wrote *The Science of Stuck*, said that it's okay to get stuck; it's not okay to stay there.

I totally agree.

But how to get unstuck? That's the bazillion dollar question, because I don't know about you, but I am capable of fretting in the same position for Quite A Long Time.

Britt's advice?

So simple it seems ridiculous…

Just move.

A teeny tiny move.

Maybe shift your body position to turn the other way.

---

[1] Episode 230 of the *You Are Not So Smart* podcast, featuring Britt Frank.

Stick a hand in the air. Kick your leg out. Uncross and recross your legs.

Better: get up and dance.

It's a variation on my theme of: make it so small you can't fail.

Don't try to get unstuck by trying to do all of the thing you're stuck on.

Simply move a body part. Start there. Change your state.

Pomodoro dancing

It's easy to think "I must move my body around more" and really difficult to actually do it.

Getting my bees all lined up and pointed in the same direction to stand up and move around is hard.

Staying in my chair is easy.

But my back hurts, so I wanted to fix this.

Enter: Pomodoro Dancing![1]

Not some kind of new flamenco class, no — it's simple.

I set a timer for 25 minutes, then when the timer goes off I ask my smart speaker to play me a song, and I dance to it and I smile and I don't care what I look like because nobody can see me, and by the time I sit down again I have new thoughts and connections and I feel like doing *all the things*.

---

[1] At the time of writing, I'm learning this dance from *The Marvelous Mrs Maisel*: https://www.youtube.com/shorts/cHJTxmcIN9s

And my body thanks me for not letting it set into the traditional Old Bent Writer position.

Try Pomodoro Dancing today.

Everything Takes longer

Me: "Oh I have 10 minutes before I have to leave for this appointment, I can write this email."

Also me: "Fuckity wasping twatnuggets I should have left 20 minutes ago WHYYYYYY."

Every. Single. Time.

I've tried everything: tracking apps, paper notes, Pomodoro timers (these are beginning to work better for me), alarms (these sometimes work), and multiple different calendars and lists.

So now I just assume this thing I am working on will take me at least three times whatever my stupid bees say it'll take.

An email in 10 minutes? HAHAHA let's say 30 to be safe.

Anothering

Speaking of being late and making up new words, here's one I literally just accidentally made up:

anothering

It's a portmanteau of "another" and "thing" because I was typing in a rush and that came out.

It perfectly describes my super annoying habit of making us late.

Here's what it means:

When you are already late, but you think you have time to do this other thing before you leave, so you try to do it, and then end up later and more stressed because YOU NEVER LEARN.

Anothering.

Time blindness

Many people aren't good at estimating how long something will take—it's called the Planning Fallacy.

But I have almost no sense of time passing—I don't know how long a minute, or an hour, or a day is. I don't know what it should *feel* like, so when I try to estimate how long something will take me, I'm wildly inaccurate—even if I've done said thing many times before.

Time blindness is a real struggle.

Joe looks at me incredulously when we have to leave in 30 minutes, and I'll reel off a list of things I just want to quickly do before we go—and each of those things will take at least 15-20 minutes. He understands, now, that I'm not *deliberately* being super annoying; I really can't figure it out.

This happens with writing, too.

Many of my days are much more stressful than they need

to be, because I pop so many things that'll "just take 10 minutes" in there.[1]

Narrator: They do not just take 10 minutes.

So it can be really helpful to run my day and week plan by Joe, because he can sense check it for me and I can adjust my expectations. And now I have Llama Life, which shows me in real-time that my list of tasks will in fact have my day finishing at 11.23 pm, instead of the 5 pm I think it's gonna be.

All this is by way of saying: writing your book, or chapter, or essay, or whatever, will almost certainly take longer than you think. And if you *do* have ADHD, your estimate may be wildly off-base.

Run your plan by someone with a little more experience[2] and writing may get a lot less stressful.

---

[1] Remember anothering?

[2] Interesting aside: I'm a whiz at helping my clients plan and structure their writing time. It's my own life I struggle with. One day I shall investigate this phenomenon.

Fun with Timers

At the time of writing, I am using an app called Llama Life which I heard about on the *Women and ADHD* podcast.[1]

I tried to use timers in the past and it'd kind of work for a few days, but then I'd forget. Or get cross with them for yelling at me.

So I tried Llama Life's timers which I love.[2] For a start, you can colour code them and add emojis.

Best of all though, I spend 5 minutes at the start of my day creating timers for everything I want to do, which shows me two things:

1. How unrealistic my expectations are when it comes to the number of things I can do in a day.

2. How long everything *really* takes me because I

---

[1] I've been a guest on there, it was great fun, look me up!

[2] The paid version of Llama Life has all sorts of cool features and is very affordable.

inevitably haven't finished by the time the timer goes off.

When I have that data, I can make more reasonable estimates and leave time for breaks and get less stressed.

Speaking of breaks—I set a timer for 5 minutes, then *dance, baby!* Sometimes I learn a TikTok dance, sometimes I practice sequences from the dance class I attend.

Either way—I'm ready to write again after moving my body.

Timers don't work for everyone, but for me they're crucial—they keep me from hyperfocusing when I have other things I need to do, like meetings.

And they keep me on track when I feel like I *just can't* because I'll set a timer for literally 1 minute, and that feels doable so I start.

AI might be awesome for ADHD writers

Remember my research methods? This probably sounds familiar to you…

I start with the thing I want to find out about, then somehow off I go, into an internet wormhole of random and slightly related topics I find interesting. On the one hand it's great, because I'm never short of ideas.

But on the other hand, I don't bloody get anything done because I'm too busy "researching." Which is why when ChatGPT thundered onto the scene, I didn't participate in the collective internet outrage. Instead, I used it—and it was gooood.

If I need to know a few facts, I'll type a question into the AI chat box and see what pops out.[1] Then I'll type another, and another—and that way, I have a good starting place for what I wanted to know and maybe a

---

[1] Check out the next chapter which is entirely written by ChatGPT. Totally unedited by me and therefore devoid of any humanity. Or fun.

couple of ideas I didn't have before. Usually it's enough to get me started writing—and give me targeted places to do more research if I want to.

No interesting but useless internet wormholes in sight. (Unless I actually decide I want an internet wormhole trek, in which case buckle up!)

ChatGPT Thoughts

Writing with ADHD can be challenging as the condition can make it difficult to focus, organize thoughts, and manage time effectively. People with ADHD may struggle with staying on task, starting projects, and following through with them.

However, with the right tools and strategies, many individuals with ADHD are able to successfully write and complete writing projects. Some tips include breaking tasks into smaller, manageable steps, using a timer to stay focused, and seeking support from a therapist or coach.

It's also important to recognize and work with one's strengths and to find writing environments that minimize distractions.

<I asked for 10 tips here.>

Sure, here are 10 tips that can help writers with ADHD:

1. Set realistic goals and break writing projects into smaller, manageable tasks.

2. Use a timer or a Pomodoro technique to stay focused for short bursts of time.

3. Minimize distractions by finding a quiet and organized workspace.

4. Use outlines, mind maps, or other pre-writing techniques to plan and organize thoughts.

5. Keep writing materials handy and accessible, such as a notebook or laptop.

6. Seek support from a therapist or coach who understands ADHD.

7. Work with your strengths and find writing methods that work best for you.

8. Take breaks frequently to stretch, move around, and refocus.

9. Reward yourself for progress and accomplishments.

10. Stay motivated by reading, networking with other writers, and setting achievable deadlines.

It's important to remember that everyone is different and may need to experiment with different strategies to find what works best. With persistence and effort, individuals with ADHD can overcome writing challenges and reach their goals.

—

Vicky is typing:

I mean, it's fine as far as it goes. Pretty standard Chad

and Brad stuff. But no real human experience, no fun, and no nuance. It's also very basic and limited.

It is, however, a place to start—I can spot all the gaps I can fill with things I've learned, I can spot where nuance is required, I can spot where I have a funny story to tell.

Give it a go, you might find it helpful.

Last-minute dot com

I do almost everything at the last minute. This is a problem due to the shame that covers me like a thin layer of slime because I know I *should* be prepared.

I *should* have written 57 drafts and edited them all meticulously.

I *should* have practised my speech 39 times in the mirror, and recorded it, and listened back to it, and learned it off by heart (with a little space for ad-libbing on the fly, natch).

I *should* have practised my trapeze routine a thousand times before my performance, smoothing out any snags, creating poetry in motion.

That's what all the experts say. And when people say to me, "Oh gosh you must have practised so hard for this," I nod and smile and blush and then walk away to find a wall to bang my head against.

So here's what I don't say out loud:

I didn't. I am not organised enough to do that. I haven't done a bazillion drafts and I don't have a thousand practices under my belt.

I don't say it out loud for two reasons.

1. People will think I'm lazy and disorganised and worst of all, that *I don't care enough about my audience to make an effort.*

2. If the thing I did was good, they'll think I'm a smug arsehole. I never share that sometimes I put out my first draft, because I know people will hate me for it *and also* I don't want people to be scared of creating something because they think writing a good first draft is how it should be.

But here's the truth I realised after a long time of feeling bad about all this:

1. I care so much about my audience and clients and readers that sometimes I think I might explode. My thoughts are mostly filled with the things I create for people.

2. It's not my first draft. Just because it's the first time it's down on paper, doesn't mean it's the first time it's existed. I've realised I write in my head: I smash out ideas and turn them into paragraphs and edit them and rewrite them and turn my ideas around. Then I put it on paper. Sometimes, it's good enough[1] to put out like that. Other times, I dive into the next stage of editing, and keep playing with it.

---

[1] Usually for social media posts, not essays or articles, and definitely not for books.

And as for trapeze, read the next story.

There is no right or wrong way to create and perform and publish in this world. If you're doing good work, and making a difference, and your method works for you, keep doing it.

By all means try something new, but don't let the world make you feel like shit if it doesn't fit you.

Doing it in my head

There's this thing I do that not everybody can do, and I never knew.

I do not have as much time as I'd like to train on my trapeze. This can become stressful when I have a competition or performance coming up, because I obviously want to create something beautiful and do it perfectly. So once I've created my routine, and I've done it a few times, I make up for my lack of *actual* training time by doing it in my head.

I didn't even realise I was doing it until my coach asked me how much I'd been practising because my routine was looking great. The truth was: not since I saw them last week. They were baffled.

What I had been doing was putting the music on a loop in my car, and doing my routine in my head while I was driving around the place.[1]

---
[1] Apparently elite athletes do this a lot. Look up Michael Phelps and his training processes.

I do this with my writing, too. And speeches, and interviews, and conversations. They all happen in my head, clear as day, over and over and over again, sometimes to the point of madness.

Maybe you do this too, and if you do, it's not only okay—it's a superpower.

Just because it doesn't look like we're working hard, doesn't mean we aren't.

Just because we haven't got 15 previous drafts there for someone to check, doesn't mean they don't exist. They're in our heads.

You are not your work

Little reminder: you are not your writing. You are worthy of love and respect even if you don't manage to write anything today.

Repeat after me:

I matter.

My work matters.

You are a wonder of evolution even if what you write isn't as good as you'd like it to be. There's always time to improve.

And on top of all that, you are the culmination of billions of years of evolution, each previous life succeeding in creating new life, beating the odds, while hurtling through space on a beautiful rock. You are literal stardust. That's pretty special, right?

On you go.

None of your business

Little reminder 2: what other people think of you is none of your business. We can't control what people think of us or our writing, which frankly sucks because I like to control as much as possible around me.[1]

It hurts when people don't like me; we're social creatures and once upon a time, our very lives depending on people liking us. Or at least, not hating us and banishing us.

But then I think: do I like everyone I meet? No.

So why should everyone like me?

The people who matter to me love me—and they love me enough to call me out on my bullshit, too, which is the most valuable love of all.[2]

---

[1] I know most control is an illusion, but it's an attractive one so shush.

[2] Of course, having said all that, I have ADHD which means I also have SUPER fun Rejection Sensitivity Dysphoria. Until I learned about this, I thought I was a pathetic little child who needed to "man up." I still struggle mightily with RSD, but I feel a little less bad about myself because of it.

Remember that next time you're worrying what strangers think of you and your work: how much do they matter to you?

Are you actually writing for them? Are they your people?

Now what about the people you're writing for?

Your work is a gift

For the longest time, I didn't publish anything at all in public. And certainly not my creative writing. And I definitely didn't submit it to publications I'd love to be published in.

[Narrator: she still doesn't send her creative writing out, despite vowing to submit three essays per month to publications.]

Why? Because I'm afraid.

If people reject my writing, surely they also reject me.

(Of course, they don't, but this isn't a logical thing it's a brain thing. And brains are rarely logical.)

Then I heard a woman interviewed on a podcast.[1] An actual rocket scientist—Dr Renee Horton. She was talking about dating—about her struggles to date in a world that still gets intimidated by intelligent, successful, ambitious women. Times by ten for accomplished Black

---

[1] *The Secret Lives of Black Women*. It's not running any new episodes anymore, but wander through the ones that are there. It's cracking.

women. She talked about letting go of the outcome and thinking of her love as a gift, and I loved that.

So now, when I write, I write for my reader of course but I also write for me, because I want to, because I love it, and I offer my writing up to the world as a gift. I can't control how people receive it. I can't make them love what I write, or even like it, or agree with it. But I can create it and offer it up, and let it go.

When I let go of the outcome, I wrote more. And I enjoyed myself more. And, I think, my writing became more vivid, funnier, more poignant… because I no longer had this uncontrollable goal. I could play, and practise in public, and see what happens.

And maybe, by the time you read this, I'll have sent my essay on cheese to some publications I'd love to be featured in.

Sit in discomfort

Art doesn't happen without discomfort. And yet, so few of us are willing to sit in our discomfort or negative feelings (including me). If we aren't willing to face down our discomfort, though, we won't create.

The creators, the prolific writers and artists, are comfortable—or at least willing—to sit in their discomfort and boredom… And use it.

Writing is uncomfy because we don't know how it's going to be received. People might hate it; and us.

It might not be good enough.

Well, I'm not here to tell you everyone will love you and your book will be amazing; they might not and it might be… less than you hope.

But we have to write anyway. That's the secret. The only secret.

Accept that we might fall short and create it anyway. It's the only way we will create things we're proud of.

Fin.

Finishing a piece of writing is always odd, for me. I have this unsettling, nagging feeling that I've left the keys in the front door, or forgotten to put the TinySheep back into their paddock.[1]

Like I've somehow missed the point of all this.

Maybe it's a hangover from the idea of "writing must be tortuous" and "all art is pain"—if writing a book isn't like Sisyphus pushing his giant rock up a hill until the end of time, surely something is wrong.

Really, though, I think it's because what I've written isn't perfect. It's very far from perfect. It's covered in cracks. And everything in my schooling and formative years drilled into me that we are aiming for *no mistakes*. Perfection is the only thing that is acceptable. Above all, we must not get it wrong, and especially not in front of people with eyeballs.

And that's the thing that holds so many of us back.

---

1 To be fair, both these things happen a lot, so that's not surprising.

We don't fit neatly, we often struggled with school, with overachievement or underachievement, with impossibly high standards (mostly set by ourselves) and so the idea of releasing something imperfect into the world is terrifying.

So I'm just going to leave you with these words from Leonard Cohen:

> "There is a crack in everything,
>
> that's how the light gets in."

Write your imperfect story. Let the light in.

Thank you

This little book was hiding with a bundle of other unfinished books. I started it on February 1, 2023, then stopped on March 2 at 7,153 words. There it would have stayed, listening to me say I was going to pick it up again but not actually doing it. Until Margo Aaron and Kristin Hatcher started their *#showyourworkchallenge* and I joined in. Every single day in May 2023, I worked on this MicroBook for a minimum of 10 minutes, and now here it is. So thank you Margo and Kristin for setting that challenge and inviting me along. This book is here now because of you.

And thank you to Misty Santos, without whom MicroBooks wouldn't even be a thing at all.

Thank you to Sarah Silva for reading an early draft of this MicroBook and helping me to make it "better."[1]

Thank you to Sarah Bartlett for asking me, one time,

---

[1] Specifically: making sure I fixed things that were obvious to me, but not the reader. For cheerleading. And for suggesting that I make it more obvious this MicroBook is for writers, and all creatives might find it useful.

years ago, "Do you have ADHD?" and sending me into a spin and onto a journey of discovery. Thank you to John Holcroft for pushing me to get an ADHD diagnosis and giving me so much insight into your experiences with this way of being. Thank you to Daniel Lee Morgan for being my absolute weirdo ADHD buddy who just gets me, and lets me be weird too.

Thank you to Edd Fletcher, who writes haiku with me almost every Friday.

Thank you to my MicroBook Magic alumni who inspired me with their MicroBooks, so I got off my arse and wrote mine: Ailene Cuthbertson, Tanja Madsen, Kelly Schrank, Johanna McWeeney, Meera Jethwa, Sandra Began, Mary Ann Skaro, Asmara Kazmi, Bridget Badoe, Sigute Zitikyte, Nick Smith, Hillary Weiss Presswood, Clara Callís Lewis, Sara Walka, Sophie Blackmore, Sarah Milne, Yinka Ewola, Sharon Blue, Misty Santos, Jill Robinson, Sarah Silva, Adefunke Larigo, Dr Nupi Arora, Kim Krause Schwalm, Victoria Veldhoen, Anaïs Bock, Maj Seider.

And, as always, thank you to Joe. For everything. And especially for making sure I don't starve to death.

Also by this author (that's me):

Business For Superheroes

How the Hell Do You Write a Book?

Banish the Blank Page of Doom

That's What She Said (exclusive Audible original)

Find me on...

Instagram @tinybeetlesteps

LinkedIn: Vicky Quinn Fraser

—

For tips, articles, and musings on writing and publishing a book, you can join my newsletter here:

moxiebooks.co.uk/notes-in-the-margin

And for my creative writing—my memoirish in progress—you can join my Substack here:

moxiebooks.substack.com

And you can listen to my podcast here:

moxiebooks.co.uk/podcast

Shenanigans

MicroBook Magic

This, as you might have noticed, is a MicroBook. A teeny tiny book all about a single simple idea. I had great fun writing it (for the most part); it takes the pressure off, and I deliberately set out for it to be fun, a bit silly, a little whimsical... but ultimately with a message that's important to me.

When I started banging on about MicroBooks in October 2022, I seem to have hit a bit of a chord with people. A bunch of writers (and people who wouldn't have called themselves writers before) joined me for a month to write their own MicroBooks.

Now, I run MicroBook Magic three or four times a year.

If you'd like to join me, you can find out when the next one is happening and join the waiting list at:

moxiebooks.co.uk/microbookmagic

Creative Playground

Back in spring 2020, when we were all wondering if we'd ever be allowed out again, I started an online writing group called the Team Moxie Power Hours.

Then, in 2023, I changed it up a bit. I noticed people weren't just writing in these sessions; some were drawing, some were learning new languages, some were dancing, some were creating products or courses. Everyone was doing something creative, so I decided to expand the boundaries and make it a Creative Playground.

Creativity is creativity, and it all feeds into each other—we find inspiration every day in what we're doing together.

Come and join us.

There are two sessions per day to choose from (attend as many as you like) and you can try it out for just £1 for the first week.

moxiebooks.co.uk/creativeplayground

Finally...

If you've enjoyed this MicroBook, please let me know!

You can leave a review on Amazon or wherever you bought the book (and if you do I will be forever grateful because reviews are like the best, most crumbly chocolate chip cookies for writers).

Or you can email me: vicky@moxiebooks.co.uk

I would love to hear from you: tell me your stories, struggles, neurodivergent tips and tricks, or just rock up and say hey.

www.ingramcontent.com/pod-product-compliance
Lightning Source LLC
Chambersburg PA
CBHW071721020426
42333CB00017B/2348